Time Out

for

Holiness

at *Work*

Other Time Out for Women books by Julie Baker
Time Out for Holiness at Home
Time Out for Prayer
A Pebble in the Pond (available spring, 2001)

Time Out
for
Holiness
at Work

Julie Baker

Cook Communications

Faithful Woman is an imprint of
Cook Communications Ministries, Colorado Springs, Colorado 80918
Cook Communications, Paris, Ontario
Kingsway Communications, Eastbourne, England

TIME OUT FOR HOLINESS AT WORK
© 2000 by Julie Baker. All rights reserved.

Printed in the United States of America.

1 2 3 4 5 6 7 8 9 10 Printing/Year 04 03 02 01 00

Editor: Glenda Schlahta
Cover Design: Jeff Lane
Interior Design: Jeff Lane

ISBN: 0-78143-462-9

Contents

Before You Begin

This book contains ten lessons designed for group study and discussion. It is intended to be facilitated, rather than taught, so the leader doesn't need teaching experience or expertise in the subject matter. The group should plan to meet once a week; advance preparation on the part of the group members is important. Each lesson will take about an hour to complete so that it could be done on a lunch break. The following is a suggested schedule:

∽ **Welcome and self-introduction of participants**

∽ **Opening prayer**
The facilitator may open in prayer or invite someone else to do so, taking care to select someone who is comfortable praying in public.

∽ **Reflection Questions**
These questions are designed to provoke thought rather than promote discussion. However, allow time for members to share brief comments before beginning the study.

∽ **Introduction**
An overview of the passage is provided at the beginning of each lesson to help guide the thinking and discussion of the group through the study time.

∽ **Study**
This section acquaints the group with a biblical character who struggled with the topical issue. The majority of your time should be spent in the **Study**, **Another Perspective**, and **Application**.

∽ **Another Perspective**
This section brings to light other passages of Scripture that relate to the topic being studied.

⌔ Application

This is an opportunity for participants to choose a course of action that will help them implement what they have learned. The facilitator might set the tone by sharing how she plans to implement what she has learned.

⌔ Conclusion and Closing Prayer

The facilitator might summarize the lesson in her own words, transitioning into prayer time. Group members can share praise and prayer requests and then spend time praying for each other.

Tips for Group Members

The success of your study group depends on you. These suggestions will help make your time together more enjoyable and more helpful.

↷ Smile. You'll find it mirrored back.

↷ Touching makes people feel significant. Shake hands, pat arms, or give hugs to help others feel valued.

↷ Make eye contact often. It not only connotes honesty and trustworthiness, but also makes people feel significant.

↷ Come prepared. Study the lesson in advance, jot down answers to questions, concerns you have about your job, prayer requests.

↷ Honor each other's comments. Everyone's contribution is valuable. Remember that what is said in the group stays in that room.

↷ Participate in the discussion and stick to the subject. If you tend to dominate conversations, excercise self-control and practice listening to what others have to say. If you're quiet, make an effort to join in the discussion.

↷ During prayer time, share your praise and requests. You might want to jot down the prayer requests of others and pray for them during the week.

Tips for Facilitators

People learn best where they feel comfortable and welcome and where their needs are being considered. Keeping the following in mind will help you provide that atmosphere.

🖝 Smile. You'll find it mirrored back.

🖝 Touching makes people feel significant. Shake hands, pat arms, or give hugs to help participants feel welcome and valued.

🖝 Make eye contact often. It not only connotes honesty and trustworthiness, but also makes people feel significant.

🖝 Did you know it takes eleven positive comments to erase one criticism? Your compliment may be the only kind word your participants hear that day! Have a policy in the group that no one is put down for her contributions. Make your study group a safe, inviting place for women to talk about their work-related concerns.

🖝 Establish a policy of confidentiality. What is said in the group stays in that room.

🖝 Encourage everyone to participate in discussion. Use open-ended questions: Why do you think that? What do you mean by . . . ? Give an example. Draw the quieter women into discussion, and help those who dominate the discussion to exercise control.

🖝 During prayer time, encourage each woman to offer one praise; then allow the needs of the group to surface. Group members might want to jot down the prayer requests so that they can pray for them during the week.

🖝 Ask the Holy Spirit to give you discernment regarding the needs in the group. A midweek phone call for progress on a prayer request goes a long way toward making people feel cared for.

⤚ The room arrangement can make people feel either included or lectured to. Arrange seating in such a way as to create a feeling of intimacy and inclusion.

⤚ Everyone appreciates organization. Stick to the time limit and come fully prepared.

⤚ Take time during the week to pray specifically for your Bible study group: for individual and group needs, as well as for the overall goal of insight into God's Word.

Introduction

Holiness. It's hard enough to maintain a degree of it in our relationships at home and with other Christians. But at work, where the values of the company and the people around us so often run contrary to Christian ideals, the challenge can be tremendous. Especially when you add into the mix our own desires to succeed and be noticed and rewarded.

There is help, however. Whether you wrestle with organization or integrity, if you struggle with motivation or a second-string position, you're not alone. In fact, your battles are age old. The Bible offers biographies of others who have been there, letting us see their failures and successes and offering us strategies that really work.

Before you begin this study, let me take just a moment to pray for you:

Dear Father God, I thank You for the women who have chosen to study Your Word and apply its truths to their work situations. I pray that they will become wise in decision making, adept at problem solving, and intuitive in their relationships. Bless them, Lord, so that they can grow in the truth and holiness of Your Word and so that their lives will be a blessing to those they touch each day. Help them, please, to always be aware of who their real boss is!

In Jesus' name, Amen.

Julie Baker

ONE

Gaining and Maintaining Respect

*S*ometimes it seems that if we want the respect of our coworkers, we need to do the things that make us look good, even if that means compromising our values. Who hasn't faced the temptation to take credit for ideas that weren't entirely ours? Or to drop names, or to buddy up to a boss? But Daniel's story shows us that the best way to gain respect—and maintain it—is to do the things that are good, not that merely look it.

Reflection Questions

Is there a particular person in your workplace whom you especially respect? What about him or her do you admire?

Do you feel that you are respected on the job? For what reasons?

Introduction

If anyone in the Bible is a model for gaining and maintaining respect, it's Daniel. Taken captive by Nebuchadnezzar as a young boy, he quickly gained the king's favor because of his ability to interpret dreams (see Daniel 2). After Nebuchadnezzar's death, however, he was apparently forgotten, because the new king, Belshazzar, had to be reminded of him (5:10-12). Again his ability to interpret visions was called upon, and again it was rewarded by a high position in the kingdom. However, his enemies were determined to get rid of him, and they devised a plot to that end. It is in the face of this plot that we see Daniel's integrity and holiness at its best, and it is from his example that we can learn how to gain and maintain the respect of others.

Study

Read Daniel 5 and 6 together.

1. Why do you think Daniel initially turned down the offer of a reward for his services?

2. Daniel did end up working for Belshazzar (very temporarily) and then for Darius. It is obvious, however, that he regarded the Lord as his true boss. In what ways did that affect the way he was viewed by his earthly boss, Darius?

↩ In what ways did it affect the way he was viewed by his coworkers?

3. Daniel 6:3 says that Daniel "began distinguishing himself among the commissioners and satraps because he possessed an extraordinary spirit" (NASB). From the story, what character traits do you think were involved in this description?

4. Daniel's story ends well, but there were surely times when he thought it wouldn't. When do you think he might have wondered about the outcome? How did he handle those times?

5. How, where, and when did Daniel display his godliness?

6. Daniel's name means "God is my judge."[1] How do we see the appropriateness of this name:

 In Daniel's actions?

 In the events of the story?

7. What impact did Daniel's character have on the people around him?

⌒ Darius:

⌒ The commissioners and satraps:

⌒ Ultimately, the entire kingdom:

Another Perspective

If Daniel provides us a role model for gaining and maintaining the respect of others, the Book of Proverbs could be considered a how-to manual for holiness. Look up the following passages. What character traits does the writer urge us to develop?

⌒ Proverbs 3:3-4

∽ Proverbs 3:27-35

∽ Proverbs 4:7-9

∽ Proverbs 10:9

∽ Proverbs 10:26

∽ Proverbs 13:18

∽ Proverbs 16:7

⤚ Proverbs 17:27

⤚ Proverbs 20:11

Application

1. From your observations, what character traits earn the respect of your coworkers?

⤚ Are these traits the same or different from the ones that earned Daniel respect?

2. What kinds of character traits earn the camaraderie of your coworkers?

↝ Are any of these traits at odds with Daniel's character qualities?

3. Is it possible to be both liked and respected by your coworkers? Discuss.

4. This story has a happy ending. Is there always a happy ending when we serve God rather than man? Give examples to support your answer.

5. If you are currently serving God, what part of your own story are you in right now? Are you experiencing a happy ending, or are you experiencing difficulties because of your faith? Give some reasons for your answer.

6. What place does faith have in the workplace? How is it best displayed?

7. Which of Daniel's character qualities do you think people see in you at work?

8. Which qualities do you think you need to work on?

Conclusion

We live in a world where biblical values are not the norm. Our coworkers are likely to be primarily looking out for number one, and that often leaves us feeling as if we need to look out for number one as well, since no one else is going to! But Proverbs 2:7-8 tells us, God "is a shield to those who walk in integrity. . . . He preserves the way of His godly ones" (NASB).

There are probably many times every day when sticking to your values is difficult. Perhaps it is when you are asked to take unethical actions, concealing the evidence of misused funds or helping a boss hide his affair, for example. More likely, however, it's in the small things—such as joining in on the jokes about a particularly annoying coworker, or overstating your progress on a certain project. These are the things we all struggle with. Take some time now to pray for each other, asking God to help you in these little daily decisions that make or break our integrity.

Memory Verse

"Let love and faithfulness never leave you; bind them around your neck, write them on the tablet of your heart. Then you will win favor and a good name in the sight of God and man" (Prov. 3:3-4).

1 Charles C. Ryrie, *Ryrie Study Bible* (Chicago: Moody Press, 1978), 1,305.

TWO

Working with Difficult People

*V*irtually no one escapes the frustration of working with difficult people. Whether it's their personality or their work habits that get on your nerves, at one time or another there's bound to be someone who rubs you the wrong way. There are many Bible characters who could probably relate, but Moses is the most likely candidate. The Book of Exodus contains page after page of the Israelites' complaints and blunders under his leadership; reading it, you wonder why he didn't throw up his hands and walk off the job— or at least demand a better crew. But human and imperfect as he was, he didn't. And in this small portion of his story, we'll get some ideas about how to deal with difficult people with an attitude of holiness, whether you're the boss or an employee.

Reflection Questions

Do you find it difficult to get along with any of your coworkers?

How do you usually approach your dealings with them? (Confrontation, avoidance, venting to other coworkers, for example.)

Introduction

The Book of Exodus tells the story of the Israelites' escape from captivity under the leadership of Moses. Its title literally means *way out*—something many of us long for as we face difficulties in our working relationships! Moses, too, had problems on the job. Like many of us, he was a go-between—not the ultimate boss, but the boss's representative in many situations. In our story, we'll see what happens when he gives responsibility to someone who does not prove trustworthy. We'll also see him responding to disloyalty on the part of the Israelites and intervening on their behalf before his Boss, the Lord God.

Study

Read together Exodus 32:15-35.

1. When Moses returned from his lengthy meeting with God, he found the Israelites worshiping an idol they had made in his absence. What was his first reaction? Do you think it was appropriate or inappropriate? (See also Mark 11:15-17; Col. 3:8; Eph. 4:26.)

2. The disciplinary action Moses took was pretty drastic, and he appears to speak for the Lord without first consulting Him. Why do you think he felt confident in doing so? Does it appear that the Lord approved or disapproved of what he did?

3. Moses apparently held Aaron responsible for what happened while he was away. Why? Do you think he was right or wrong in doing so? Explain why you think so.

4. There's no doubt that Aaron had some pretty difficult people to work with in Moses' absence. There's also not much doubt that he handled the situation poorly. How do you think Aaron should have handled these situations:

⬿ When the people wondered why Moses hadn't returned?

⬿ When confronted by Moses?

5. The next day Moses went to talk to the Lord about what had happened. How do you think he felt as he approached that meeting? Why might he have waited a day?

6. What do you think of the way Moses handled the conversation with the Lord? Why would he take that approach?

Another Perspective

You don't have to read far in the Bible before realizing that relationships are important to God. And as Christians, we often have the impression that God wants us to slap a smile on our face and do whatever it takes to keep our relationships running smoothly. But think about it for a moment. As much as God loves all of us, and as much as He desires to be close to each one of us, doesn't He place limits on how He allows us to behave? Aren't there times when He draws a line on our behavior? Taken as a whole, the Scriptures offer us a balance in how we respond to difficult people. They also show us that different responses are called for in different circumstances—and while we cannot be responsible for the behavior of others, we are held accountable for our own.

Look up the following passages and discuss how they relate to dealing with difficult people.

≈ Psalm 34:14

≈ 1 Thessalonians 5:14-15

≈ Matthew 5:9

~ Proverbs 14:29

~ Ephesians 4:26

~ 1 Peter 4:9

~ Psalm 26:5

~ Proverbs 17:14

~ Psalm 1:1

Based on these passages, how would you handle the following scenarios?

↷ One of your coworkers uses language that you find offensive, but you're aware that others most likely don't.

↷ You feel that you are carrying the majority of the workload while others slack off.

↷ A couple of your coworkers tend to joke about some of your least-favorite people behind their backs, and their remarks are genuinely funny. You find yourself being drawn into these conversations.

Application

1. Is your job description more like that of Moses, Aaron, or the Israelites?

2. In your job, have you experienced:

↷ A coworker who constantly grumbles and complains about your boss?

↶ Being left with responsibility you felt unable to handle?

↶ Leaving someone in charge who lets you down?

Describe the situation and how you handled it.

Having read this story, are you pleased with how you handled it, or do you think you could have approached it in a more holy way? Explain your answer.

3. Does any part of your behavior at work resemble that of the Israelites? In what ways?

↶ If so, what could you do to change this?

4. Does any part of your behavior at work resemble that of Aaron? In what ways?

⤝ If so, what could you do to change this?

5. Does any part of your behavior resemble that of Moses? Do you view this as positive or negative?

6. Based on this study, is there anything you would like to change about the way you deal with difficult people? What is a first step you can take this week to make that change?

Conclusion

Personality clashes go with the territory when you have a group of people working together. We need to avoid contributing to the problem; as Paul says, "If it is possible, as far as it depends on you, live at peace with everyone"(Rom. 12:18). But when the trouble goes beyond personality clashes to persistent grumbling, misconduct, or mistreatment of people, it's time to decide on a course of action. Pray for each other, asking God to give each of you the wisdom you need to know how to handle the situations you face.

Memory Verse

"The fear of the Lord is the beginning of knowledge;
fools despise wisdom and instruction" (Prov. 1:7, NASB).

THREE

Dealing with a Difficult Boss

~⁓)⁓

*D*ealing with a difficult boss is—well, difficult! And it's an experience that most of us are likely to face sooner or later. The difficulties may arise from a personality clash, from chronic miscommunication, or from a myriad of other sources . . . but the solution is the same for them all. Today we will examine the story of a man named Obadiah, who had a boss far worse than any we are ever likely to have, and we'll see how he responded to a bad situation.

Reflection Questions

Do you now have, or have you ever had, a boss who is difficult to work for? In what ways is this so?

How does, or did, the situation impact your work or your feelings about work?

Introduction

Obadiah held a high position in the palace of King Ahab. Why he stayed in it, we don't know—Ahab was a terrible boss, ungodly and violent. Death awaited any who crossed him. We can speculate that Obadiah stayed in his job out of self-preservation; since Samaria was in the throes of a terrible drought, if anyone had access to food and water, it would have been Ahab. Whatever the reason, it is clear from our passage that Obadiah had torn loyalties. Sometime earlier, he had saved one hundred prophets from the wrath of Jezebel, Ahab's wife, by hiding them in caves and bringing them bread and water. But now, asked by the Prophet Elijah to tell Ahab that Elijah has come, we can almost see him shaking in his sandals, because Ahab despises Elijah. In fact, Elijah has been at the top of Ahab's most-wanted list for three years, and Obadiah is sure that if he brings the message, his fate will be death by association. Let's see how he deals with this most difficult of bosses.

Study

Read together 1 Kings 18:1-16.

1. How would you describe Obadiah?

2. How would you describe Ahab?

3. Why do you think Obadiah risked his life to save the prophets?

4. After that earlier show of courage and character, why do you think Obadiah is now so fearful of conveying Elijah's message?

5. What do you think finally convinced Obadiah to do as Elijah asked?

6. Which aspects of Obadiah's attitude toward his boss do you think were positive?

≈ Which aspects do you think were not positive?

Another Perspective

Obadiah appears to be doing the best he can in an impossible situation—like many of us. Fortunately, we have a resource he didn't have. Many of the writers of the New Testament address the tough issues that employees face and give us advice on how to handle them with holiness. One of the best known passages on the subject is Colossians 3:22-25. Take some time to read it and respond to the following questions.

↷ According to this passage, what qualities should characterize our work?

↷ Colossians 4 goes on to address the attitudes and actions expected of masters—or bosses. If a boss does not meet those expectations, are we released from the expectations of slaves—or employees—described earlier? Why or why not?

↷ Whom do you think Colossians 3:25 is referring to? How does that verse make you feel?

Now read Ephesians 6:5-8.

↷ What do you think is the difference between doing your job to please your boss and doing it to serve the Lord?

↷ Surely God knows that our earthly bosses are not always godly. Why do you think He insists that we obey them and treat them with respect?

◦ Why do you think it is easier to do your job well if you are doing it for the Lord than if you are doing it for your earthly boss?

Romans 12:9-21 gives us some brief and to-the-point instructions on how Christians are to treat each other. Even though your boss may not be a Christian, much of this advice could help you smooth the rough waters of your relationship and discern where to draw lines in the sand. Read this passage and comment on the verses you think are particularly applicable.

Drawing on what you've studied, discuss how you might handle the following scenarios.

◦ Your boss tells you to do a job a certain way; then, when the task is almost complete, he or she changes the direction and aim of the project. Now your previous work has been wasted; worse, the results will now be late and you are likely to be blamed. How should you handle this?

◦ Your boss socializes with several employees whose rank and responsibilities are the same as yours, and you frequently feel left out of the loop of information that has evidently been shared over cocktails or a golf game. What's more, you suspect that his affinity for these people causes you to be passed over for choice assignments. What should you do?

Application

1. In what ways can you relate to Obadiah's dilemma? What would you have done in his shoes?

2. Do you find it difficult to have the kind of holy attitude toward work described in Colossians and Ephesians? Why or why not?

3. What is the most difficult aspect of your relationship with your boss at this time? What that you've read or discussed today seems relevant or applicable to your situation? How is it relevant or applicable?

4. Do you tend to think of your boss merely as a boss or as a person with needs and struggles? What kinds of needs and struggles do you think your boss might be facing at this time?

5. What, if any, part of your attitude toward your boss could use changing? What might help you make this change? (Prayer, Scripture memory, support of friends, for example.)

Conclusion

It's unlikely any of us will ever have a boss as difficult as Obadiah's! But all of us can probably see ourselves in some aspect of his story. Who hasn't been stuck in an unpleasant job because of the need for a paycheck? Who hasn't been torn between self-preservation and doing the right thing? Who hasn't felt inwardly sympathetic to the causes of those on the other side of an issue from our boss?

No matter what our situation at work, we can be comforted in this: God loves us and knows every detail of our struggle. He would like nothing more than to be called upon for help. And who knows, He may even have some pleasant surprises in store—ones we'll experience only if we trust and obey His Word!

Memory Verse:
"Whatever you do, work at it with all your heart, as working for the Lord, not for men" (Col 3:23).

FOUR

Handling Office Politics

ffice politics—it's a game everyone hates, but one that few dare stay out of! Consciously or unconsciously, we're all aware that, no matter how good we are at our job, our chances for promotion are higher if we participate in the politics. Whether that means angling for high-profile projects or schmoozing with the right people or playing up to the boss, most of us have struggled to walk the fine line between just doing our job and doing what's best for our image. And many of us have resented the necessity of having to think that way. What we'd really like is to be left alone to do our job and not have to worry about how we're being perceived—or what others are doing to promote themselves. But is that realistic?

Reflection Questions

Are office politics a necessary evil, or is it possible—or smart—to avoid them?

Have you witnessed a colleague receiving a promotion that you suspected was based more on politics than on talent or experience? What effect did that have on you? On your coworkers?

Introduction

Our story today is told in two different passages by two different eyewitnesses. Both writers observed their boss handle two brown-nosing brothers who actually brought their mother along to help their case! The boss is Jesus, and the brothers are two of the disciples—men you'd think would know better. But, like all of us at times, they temporarily lost sight of the job at hand and set their eyes on getting ahead. Let's see how Jesus responds.

Study

Read together Mark 10:35-45 and Matthew 20:20-28.

1. Part of playing the politics game is determining which way the wind is blowing and trying to get there ahead of everyone else. Obviously, James and John (and their mother) saw Jesus as an up-and-coming leader and wanted to position themselves to share the glory when it came. Describe leadership as you think the disciples were envisioning it.

2. Judging from Jesus' reply, what do you think true leadership looks like?

3. Many bosses would be flattered to have people so obviously wanting to be associated with them. Others might be merely annoyed. How do you think Jesus felt about it?

4. As it always does, word of what James and John had done got around. Both passages describe the reaction of the other disciples as indignation. Why do you think they felt that way? Was it an appropriate reaction?

5. Why do you think Jesus called everyone together for a meeting? What might He have been trying to avoid, and what do you think He hoped to accomplish?

Another Perspective

The Book of Proverbs is a rich resource for how to handle office politics with holiness. Chapter 16, in particular, offers us some important insights.

Successful careers don't just happen; they take hard work and planning. But there is a difference between planning and scheming.

🔊 Read verses 1-3, 9, 25, and 33. What do these tell us about our plans?

🔊 Read verses 5 and 18-19. What attitude does God honor, and what does He despise? How does this relate to the work environment?

➥ According to verses 21, 23-24, and 27-28, how can our conversations and tone of voice affect the atmosphere of the office and people's perception of us?

➥ It may seem as though the only way to get ahead at work is to look out for number one, but what perspective do verses 8, 11, and 17 give to this notion?

➥ If you are the boss, verses 12-13 have some special advice for you. What is it?

Application

1. Proverbs 16:16 tells us that it is more important to gain wisdom than money. If that truly became the order of your priorities, how might it affect your life, both at home and at work?

2. Jesus demonstrated that a true leader is really a servant. How could you play the role of servant at work? Get specific.

3. Of the all the things we discussed today regarding holiness in the face of office politics, which is the most difficult for you to apply? How can your group help or pray for you in this matter?

4. Others in your office may be acting out of fear and the need to protect their interests and their territory. From our study, you know that you do not need to do this; you have the Lord looking out for you! Instead of reacting in kind, try praying for them. In time, they may begin to mirror your relaxed attitude.

Conclusion

Today's work environment can seem like a cutthroat world where only the most aggressive succeed. If your workplace is not like that, count yourself blessed! But if it is, know that God is your champion, working behind the scenes on your behalf. No, He doesn't necessarily promise you worldly achievement. But He does promise to provide for you (Matt. 6:25-26) . . . and beyond that, to "satisf[y] your years with good things" (Ps. 103:5, NASB). That satisfaction, however, is something you'll miss out on unless you align your priorities with His and let holiness permeate your heart, whether at home or at work.

Memory Verse

"Whoever wants to become great among you must be your servant, and whoever wants to be first must be your slave" (Matt. 20:26-27).

FIVE

Developing Appropriate Working Relationships

For better or for worse, we spend a good portion of our waking hours at work. So naturally, the people we work with often become a significant part of our lives. Elsewhere in our lives, by and large, we are able to choose the people we spend time with. At work, those people are chosen for us. How we relate to them plays a significant role in how much we enjoy our jobs, yet it is often difficult to determine what constitutes an appropriate working relationship. And when coworkers become friends, it can affect the quality of our work—either positively or negatively. Today we'll examine how holiness can help us as we navigate the sometimes tricky trails of working relationships.

Reflection Questions

Have you ever been in a work environment where personal relationships got in the way of getting the work done? Describe the situation.

Have you ever been in a work situation in which tense relationships negatively affected the quality of work being done? Describe what was happening.

Introduction

Our story today is about Joseph, who was the son of Jacob, who was the son of Isaac, who was the son of Abraham. Joseph was one of the twelve brothers who became heads of the twelve tribes of Israel. His brothers, however, were not crazy about him, primarily because he was his father's favorite. Unbearably jealous and resentful, they threw him into a pit, sold him as a slave, and told their father he was dead. Joseph was taken to Egypt and sold as a slave to Potiphar, who was so pleased with him that he kept promoting him until finally Joseph was the head of Potiphar's entire household. That cushy position was not without its pitfalls, however, particularly in the area of relationships. Let's take a look at the problem Joseph faced and how he handled it.

Study

Read together Genesis 39:1-23.

1. As a foreigner and a slave, how was Joseph able to work his way into such a high position?

⌒ What character qualities do you think Joseph must have possessed in order to have been given charge over everything Potiphar owned?

2. Describe the problem Joseph faced with Potiphar's wife. Was there anything Joseph could have done to have avoided the problem?

3. What about Joseph's treatment of the problem was good?

⮑ What might he have done differently, if anything?

4. Look at Joseph's response to Potiphar's wife in verses 8-9. Does the last line surprise you? Why is the last word *God* and not *Potiphar*?

5. Potiphar's wife's behavior and lies obviously affected Joseph's life. Take a moment to speculate how her actions might also have affected the rest of her household.

6. Joseph was treated unfairly twice so far that we know of—first, his brothers hated him because of something his father did wrong; second, he was thrown in jail because of something Potiphar's wife did wrong. The text says several times, though, that "the Lord was with him" (vv. 2, 3, 21, 23). Why do you think God did not prevent these wrongs from occurring?

Another Perspective

Working relationships can be a blessing or a curse. Handled appropriately, they can keep us motivated and stimulate us to achieve more than we would otherwise. They can even blossom into true friendships. But handled inappropriately, they can destroy our working environment and even our lives and those of others. A million temptations face us every day: the temptation to let a friendship slip into flirtation—or more; the temptation to let friendships influence work-related decisions; the temptation to gossip about things you can't help but learn in such close and constant quarters . . . the list goes on and on. But the rules governing Christian relationships apply to work relationships as well. Colossians 3 is full of good advice. Comment on the relevance of the following verses.

🔖 v. 5

🔖 v. 8

🔖 vv. 9-11

🔖 vv. 12-13

≈ vv. 14-15

≈ v. 17

≈ v. 23

Discuss the following scenarios and brainstorm ways you might handle them.

≈ Your coworker seems to know everything about everyone and is only too happy to let you in on their secrets. You don't want to listen to gossip, but neither do you want to alienate her. What do you do?

≈ A rumor is going around that you are privately seeing the good-looking guy in the office around the corner. It is untrue; he is merely a friend whom you know well from church, and both of you are in committed marriages. No matter what you say, though, the rumor persists. What do you do?

Application

1. Are you involved in any relationships at work that might be construed as inappropriate? Think about the following categories:

⌒ Friendships in which conversations regularly infringe on your work time.

⌒ Friendships that cause others to feel left out.

⌒ Friendships that may be causing you to act out of favoritism or to be unduly influenced in work-related decisions.

⌒ Friendships that are inappropriately crossing a line into romantic feelings, even if only playfully.

⤳ Friendships that use work time for matters—even important ones—best taken care of during nonwork hours, such as witnessing, Bible study, or friend-to-friend counsel.

2. What are some policies you could implement in your work relationships that could prevent improprieties from occurring? For example: cutting personal conversations short with an invitation to continue during lunch; keeping the door open during meetings with people of the opposite sex.

3. If the atmosphere in your office is strained, what practical things can you do to ease the tension and foster friendship?

4. When your relationships are misconstrued, as Joseph's was, and nothing you do or say changes the perception, in what can you take comfort?

Conclusion

Good working relationships can mean the difference between a job you dread and one you enjoy. But the balance between propriety and impropriety can be delicate; pitfalls abound. Ask God to help you maintain that balance. Examine your actions and see if they are holy. Are they contributing to the general good of the workplace? Do they contribute to positive morale? Do they point the way to the Savior, or do they obscure it? It's hard not to succumb to gossip and cliquishness and backbiting, but with the Holy Spirit inside you, all things are possible.

Memory Verse

"And whatever you do, whether in word or deed, do it all in the name of the Lord Jesus, giving thanks to God the Father through him" (Col. 3:17).

SIX

Making Wise Decisions

ll of us make decisions all day long. Many are small—which shoes to wear with which outfit or where to go for lunch—but some have far-reaching consequences. Which job to take? What church to attend? Whom to marry? On the job decisions abound as well, and many of them affect other people. Sometimes making those decisions can be paralyzing. How does holiness enter into decision making? Are there biblical guidelines for approaching decisions? Let's read on to find out.

Reflection Questions

Which decisions are harder: the ones you make at home or the ones you make at work? Why?

Do you approach decision making differently at work than you do at home? In what ways?

Introduction

Today, we'll look at the stories of two men. In one of them, we'll see the value Solomon placed on wisdom to make decisions. In the other, we'll see the consequences of Joshua's unwise decision and what could have prevented it.

Study

First, read together 1 Kings 3:1-15.

1. Solomon is known as the wisest man who ever lived. What was the source of his wisdom?

2. If we were given one wish, most of us would probably wish for a smaller dress size, a bigger house, or a million dollars. What do you think prompted Solomon to make the request he did?

3. What does God's response to Solomon's request show us about His desires for us?

4. What character qualities are evidenced in Solomon's request?

5. Read 1 Kings 3:16-28. How did Solomon exercise his God-given wisdom in this situation?

Now read together Joshua 9:1-16.

1. As this story begins, Joshua and his people are riding high on victory. With God's miraculous help, they had recently defeated two of the tribes that inhabited Canaan, the land promised to them by God. With such success behind them—and such proof of the importance of God's involvement—why do you think they neglected to invite Him into this decision?

2. God's plan was for the Israelites to take full possession of the Promised Land. Why do you think He didn't intervene and prevent the treaty from being made?

3. What character qualities did Joshua display in the events of this story?

Another Perspective

Decision making has been a concern of people since the beginning of recorded history. In the Old Testament, the Lord set up a method by which the priests could make decisions. Exodus 28 describes in detail the garments that priests were to wear, including a breastpiece which was constructed specifically for the purpose of decision making. Over the heart of this breastpiece was a type of pocket which contained two dicelike items called Urim, representing a no answer, and Thummim, representing yes. When a decision needed to be made, the priest would ask his question and then pull out one of the dice, and this would be his answer. Sounds pretty chancey, doesn't it? But as Proverbs 16:33 reminds us, "The lot is cast into the lap, but its every decision is from the Lord."

Sometimes we wish for such a tangible answer from God! But as New Testament Christians, we now have a different way of obtaining God's insights. Go to the following passages to discover the resources we have available to us.

⮑ James 1:5

⮑ John 16:13

⮑ Colossians 2:1-3

Though the Bible never outlines a fail-safe process for making wise decisions, it's not hard to come up with some steps that are always good to follow. Use the verses that follow to determine the steps most likely to lead to sound judgment.

⇨ Step One: Joshua 9:14, 1 Kings 22:5, 2 Chronicles 18:4

⇨ Step Two: Numbers 13:17-20, Joshua 2:1, Judges 1:22-25

⇨ Step Three: Proverbs 12:15, 22, Proverbs 19:20

⇨ Step Four: Psalm 27:14, Psalm 46:10, Proverbs 19:2, Philippians 4:6-7

Application

1. Many decisions can be made very easily, simply by determining whether the choice involves violating any godly principles. For instance, should you lie for your boss? Obviously not, even though you may pay a price for making a decision for holiness. Other decisions are not moral in nature, in which case the answers are not quite so evident. Take a few moments to evaluate the nature of

the decisions that are currently troubling you—are they moral choices or amoral ones?

2. At the beginning of the lesson, you were asked whether you make decisions differently at home than at work. What was your answer? Why was this so? Do you think it should be that way?

3. List a few people in your life to whom you could go for godly counsel. If you have difficulty thinking of any, what changes do you need to make in your life so that this kind of person will be more available to you?

4. One way to determine whether or not your decision is a good one is by the presence or absence of peace. In the midst of our busy lives, however, there are often so many voices vying for our attention that we wouldn't notice a sense of peace if it flooded us. Likewise, we may attribute a sense of uneasiness to any number of things besides the real issue. Do you make time in your life to sit quietly and listen to your heart? To God? If not, where in your day could you carve out a few minutes to do so?

Conclusion

No doubt about it—making holy decisions, whether at home or in the work-place, is not easy. So many of them have long-range consequences, either for us or for someone else. But we can be sure that God knows every detail of every decision we will ever be called upon to make. He knows the potential results of every choice, and He wants to help us choose. But even if we make a mistake, He provides a safety net: "And we know that God causes all things to work together for good to those who love God, to those who are called according to His purpose" (Rom. 8:28, NASB). Isn't that good news? There is no error we can make that is beyond His redemption. So pray, research, get godly counsel, and pray some more . . . but at the same time, relax. You couldn't be in better hands.

Memory Verse
"First seek the counsel of the Lord" (1 Kings 22:5).

SEVEN

Learning to Delegate

e've been learning how to be women of character, and women of character do their jobs with excellence, right? We make sure every part of every assignment is done perfectly, even if it means working ourselves to exhaustion, coming in early, going home late, missing our children's piano recitals and soccer games. . . . You've felt that tension before, haven't you? Is it possible to be holy in the way you do your job without taxing your body and your family beyond endurance? There is a way, and we'll discover it in today's lesson.

Reflection Questions

When you feel stressed at work, how does it affect your life? Your family?

What kinds of circumstances tend to make you feel overwhelmed?

Introduction

Today's study begins with Moses, who had a big job to do, and ends with Jesus, who had an even bigger job to do. Their stories are different, though, in that Moses was trying to stretch himself far enough to cover the entire job himself—and Jesus broke the job into pieces and handed them to others. As we meet Moses today, he is fresh from experiencing some incredible miracles: the parting of the Red Sea and the provision of manna, meat, and water in the desert. His people, too, have seen these things and are eager (for now, anyway) to follow God. Not having the Bible, as we do, and aware that Moses had a pretty direct line to the Lord, they had begun swarming to Moses for advice on how to resolve their quarrels. So time-consuming was this task that Moses would go straight to his judgment seat in the morning and stay in it until evening, hearing one case after another. He was still riding pretty high from their successful escape, and no doubt he was highly motivated to help the Israelites behave in a godly manner, but his father-in-law, Jethro, saw the crash coming. Respectfully, but with the wisdom that comes with years, he gave Moses a piece of advice.

Study

Read together Exodus 18:5-27 and respond to the following questions.

1. In an earlier lesson, we learned about the Urim and Thummim, which were the decision-making dice that the priest would draw out of his breast pocket when faced with a dilemma. No one but Moses would have had access to these, so evidently there were some parts of his job that he could not delegate.[1] What principles did Jethro suggest for determining what tasks Moses could give up?

2. Giving up part of his job also meant that Moses acquired a new task. What was it, and why was it important? (See verse 20.)

3. The obvious benefit of delegating the work was that it would prevent Moses from wearing out (v. 18). Speculate on what some of the added benefits would be, not only for Moses, but for the entire group.

4. How was Moses to select the people to take on part of his work?

☞ Why were these qualities important?

☞ Would these qualities be the ones to use in any situation? Why or why not?

Read together Mark 3:13-15 and Luke 9:1-2; 10:1-3, 17-19.

1. Why do you think Jesus called first twelve and then seventy-two men to help Him?

☙ What was the difference in the type of work He wanted the twelve to do versus the seventy-two?

2. Why do you think He sent the seventy-two out in pairs?

3. What did Jesus do to ensure the success of His delegates?

Another Perspective

We've been reading about delegating tasks to others, and it's not hard to understand why that's a good idea—intellectually, anyway. In actual practice, though, we so often just keep gutting it out, gritting our teeth, and keeping at the task until we collapse. Let's venture out to a hillside and spy on a drama that gives us a visual picture of our need for help.

Read together Exodus 17:8-16.

☙ How do you think Moses felt in verses 9-11?

≈ How do you think Aaron and Hur felt?

≈ How was Moses likely feeling at the beginning of verse 12?

≈ How do you think he felt once Aaron and Hur began to help him?

≈ How do you think Aaron and Hur felt as they helped him?

≈ Why do you think God chose such an odd method of defeating an army?

Application

1. Do you have trouble asking for help, or is it something you do easily?

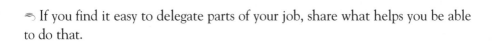 If you find it easy to delegate parts of your job, share what helps you be able to do that.

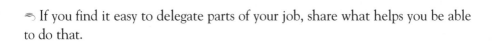 If you find it difficult to delegate, what factors cause your reluctance?

2. In the stories we read today, the men needing help were both leaders with huge responsibilities. But people at the bottom of the totem pole can get just as overwhelmed with their responsibilities. If you are at the bottom of your workplace totem pole, do these stories have any relevance for you? If you have no one to delegate to, what might you do when your arms get tired, like Moses'?

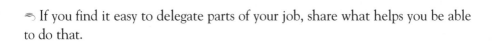 What tends to prevent you from asking for help?

3. How do you respond when you are on the receiving end of the delegation of work? If your attitude could use some adjustment, how will this lesson help you with this week's tasks?

4. It's one thing to admit you need to ask for help; it's another thing to actually do it! The following exercise might help.

≈ Make a list of the tasks you are responsible for at work.

≈ Cross off the ones that can truly be done only by you.

≈ With the items remaining, pray that God will help you see ways to spread these tasks among others.

≈ If you have the authority to do so, consider the nature of each task and decide who is best suited to take each one on.

↶ Pray about ways to bring the matter up to these people, who may or may not welcome taking on another task. Or, if applicable, pray about ways to talk to your boss about the tasks you feel are overloading your schedule.

↶ Now put your best efforts into the tasks that only you can do!

Conclusion

Holiness does not mean taking on more than we can reasonably handle. Holiness does require us to work hard and to the best of our ability; it may mean that we work extra hard for short stints of time now and then. But day in and day out, our bodies and minds need rest, and our families need time with us. Over the decades, our culture has come to expect long workweeks and heavy responsibilities. And sometimes, our pride demands that we put those hours in, that we prove our capability. It can feel like an admission of weakness to ask for help. Realistically, it may even be viewed that way by our colleagues. But keeping up an impossible pace takes its toll on our health, our happiness, our relationship to God, and our personal lives and families. And letting that happen just isn't in the definition of holiness.

God was watching out for Moses when He sent Jethro with that good advice. He's watching out for you too. Let Him take care of you, won't you?

Memory Verse

"Though one may be overpowered,
two can defend themselves.
A cord of three strands is not quickly broken" (Eccl. 4:12).

---

1 F. F. Bruce, ed., *The International Bible Commentary* (Grand Rapids, Mich.: Zondervan Publishing Co., 1979), 169.

EIGHT

Becoming a Positive Problem-Solver

*I*f you are breathing, you have problems! Problems are just a way of life, whether at work or at home. But it's not really the problems themselves that are the issue—it's how you approach them. Let's look at two Bible characters who had big problems on their hands. One of them provides a great model for how to solve a problem in a positive, holy way; the other provides a perfect model to avoid!

Reflection Questions

How do you feel when problems come your way? Paralyzed? Panicked? Energized? Resolved? Describe your usual reaction.

Do you think it is or is not possible to avoid most problems? Why or why not?

Introduction

Our first story is about Aaron, Moses' brother and his right-hand man. When Moses went to Mount Sinai for a visit with God (the one that yielded the Ten Commandments), he took Joshua along with him and left Aaron and Hur in charge. Unfortunately, the Israelites were not an easy bunch to be in charge of. Even after witnessing miracle after miracle, their feet were not very firmly planted in faith. When Moses was gone longer than they expected, they gave up on him and started putting pressure on Aaron to do something. Let's see how he responded.

Read together Exodus 32:1-10.

1. Before we address Aaron's actions, let's look at how Moses might have prevented this problem to begin with. What could he have done differently that might have changed the outcome?

2. With Moses gone so long, the Israelites, never known for their patience or steadfastness, got restless. Even though God had saved them countless times, they were afraid Moses might be dead or lost or who knows what else. And restlessness in a group as large and as volatile as the Israelites were could be pretty intimidating. Describe the way you think Aaron may have been feeling.

➣ How do you think his feelings affected his actions?

How could he have handled his feelings differently?

3. Back in Exodus 24:14, we're told that Moses left both Aaron and Hur in charge, yet we don't see any mention of Hur in this story. What is significant about his absence? What do you think might have been different if he had been involved?

4. How could Aaron have handled this situation differently?

5. What does Aaron's problem-solving technique tell us about his character?

Now let's read a story about Nehemiah—but first, a little background. The Book of Nehemiah is evidently largely Nehemiah's diary[1]. In it, he tells us about his concern for the people of Israel, now returned from Babylonian exile. They were living unprotected in Jerusalem, the city walls having crumbled in their absence. So Nehemiah receives permission from his employer, King Artaxerxes I, to go and rebuild the wall, and he accomplishes this mammoth task in just fifty-two days. But his job was not without its problems (see chapters 4-6); the work was threatened from a number of sources. Today we'll just look at the way he handled the enemies who wanted to undermine his project, but the entire book is well worth studying for anyone who wants to learn how to overcome trouble and accomplish a task.

Before going on, read together Nehemiah 6:1-16.

1. One of the biggest problems we all face—but don't always recognize—is getting distracted from the task at hand. In just these few verses, Nehemiah dodged several opportunities to be sidetracked from his mission. What were they?

☞ Each of these distractions could easily have seemed important enough to warrant Nehemiah's attention. Why do you think he was able to stay on task?

2. When we're immersed in a task, it's easy to put blinders on and miss the things that are happening peripherally. But Nehemiah didn't take the messages sent his way at face value; he was incredibly perceptive about the real motives behind them. How do you think he managed to be so insightful?

3. Contrast the way Nehemiah handled problems with the way Aaron handled problems. What differences do you see?

4. What do Nehemiah's problem-solving techniques show us about his character?

Another Perspective

How do the following Scriptures relate to the stories you've just read?

≈ James 1:12

≈ James 5:16

≈ Proverbs 1:10

≈ Proverbs 10:9

⤚ Proverbs 16:3

Application

1. When Aaron was faced with a problem, his first reaction was to fall back on the familiar. If the people wanted a physical object to worship, he was going to give them one! Even if he knew it to be foolish and wrong. When you face a problem at work, what familiar crutch do you tend to rely on?

2. Many times our problems arise from the things we have allowed to distract us. Think about the most pressing task you are facing right now. What things distract you from focusing on that task? Can any of those distractions be postponed or eliminated?

3. Are you faced with any troubling issues in your job or with coworkers right now? Describe them briefly.

≈ Below, draw a large circle. Then draw another smaller circle inside the first, and finally, a third circle inside the second circle. In the smallest (center) circle, write down the problems over which you have full control. Around the outside of that circle, list the problems over which you have some control. In the outer circle, write the things over which you have no control.

≈ Which of these things should be your primary focus at this time?

4. For the problems that fall within your realm of control or influence, try implementing this strategy:
≈ First, pray for God's wisdom.

≈ Second, list the major facets of the problem.

∽ Third, outline the possible outcomes.

∽ Fourth, brainstorm several possible solutions with a trusted adviser or coworker.

∽ Fifth, decide on a course of action. If applicable, involve others who are affected by the situation.

∽ Last, solve the problem through
    a. creating a reasonable timeline
    b. implementing the planned strategy
    c. evaluating progress along the way and making any necessary adjustments
    d. trusting God with the outcome

5. For problems that fall outside your sphere of influence, fall to your knees and take them to the Father, leaving them in His capable hands. List your most pressing concerns here.

Conclusion

Wouldn't it be nice if we could clear our paths of problems? Too bad it will never happen. Or is it too bad? James tells us that we should welcome trials as friends, because it is through them that we develop maturity, which is a priceless commodity (James 1:2-4).

Memory Verse

"I can do everything through him who gives me strength" (Phil. 4:13).

---

1 Ryrie, *Ryrie Study Bible*, 710.

NINE

Preparing for Promotion

romotion. We love the sound of that word, don't we? It resonates with dreams of more prestige, more money, affirmation of our abilities . . . and the realities of more work, more responsibility, and more headaches! As Dilbert once said, "I thought I wanted a better job. Turns out I just wanted a better paycheck." Preparing for promotion doesn't just mean mentally decorating your new cubicle. It means searching your heart to see whether you really want that new position and evaluating your skills to see if you're ready. And a host of other things, which we will find out about in today's study.

Reflection Questions

When you think of your ideal job, what does it consist of? What qualifications are needed for it?

Promotion often involves competition, and businesses often have employees prepared to do anything to get to the top. Do you think it's possible to maintain a standard of holiness while holding your own on the ladder to success? Why or why not?

Introduction

In the Old Testament, the mantle of leadership was often handed over with much solemnity and, sometimes, ceremony. It was not an event to be taken lightly, and it was a shift that took place after years of preparation. In this study we will observe three occasions when leadership changed hands. We will not be able to observe all of what went before the passing of the baton, although those stories are available in the Scriptures. However, the preparation that has gone before is implied in these moments of transition. Let's see what we can glean from these accounts about what it takes to be truly prepared for promotion.

Study

Read Numbers 27:12-23 and Joshua 1.

1. Like most leaders, Moses had practiced at least one trial run at leaving someone else in charge of the unruly Israelites. That time, it was his brother, Aaron, and it was with disastrous results (see Ex. 32:1-10). When the Lord told Moses that he would not be going into the Promised Land with his people, Moses entreated God to appoint someone else to lead in his place. The man God chose was someone who had quietly shadowed Moses since the beginning of their journey—his servant Joshua. How is Joshua described in the two passages?

2. How is Moses described in Joshua 1:2?

3. In these passages, we're not given much information about Joshua's character or abilities. From what we do know of him—that he had God's spirit, and that he was Moses' servant—why do you think he was the logical choice for Moses' replacement?

Next read 1 Kings 19:19-21 and 2 Kings 2:1-15.

1. Elijah was a strong prophet of God, but after a particularly exhausting, although successful, confrontation with the priests of Baal, he felt so discouraged and alone in his spiritual battle that he wanted to die. He had simply had enough. So the Lord assured him that he was not the lone voice for righteousness; in fact, there were seven thousand left who had not bowed down to Baal. And He also let Elijah know that the end was in sight, telling him to appoint Elisha as prophet in his place (1 Kings 18:1–19:18). We have no indication, however, that the Lord gave Elisha any advance notice of this! One moment he was plowing fields; the next, he was wearing Elijah's mantle. What was Elisha's reaction (see 1 Kings 19:19-21)?

2. What did this new assignment cost Elisha?

3. Was Elisha immediately placed in a prestigious position of authority? Speculate about what his duties may have been.

4. What does the 2 Kings passage tell you about the relationship between Elisha and Elijah?

Now, read 1 Kings 2:1-12.

1. Solomon was not David's only son. We are not told he chose Solomon to take the throne, but, given David's speech and the results of Solomon's reign (see verse 12), speculate on why David might have selected Solomon.

2. From what David said to Solomon, do you think he expected Solomon to carry on the work he (David) had begun, or was he giving Solomon carte blanche to reign as he pleased?

3. Does it appear that Solomon honored David's request?

Another Perspective

In our culture, success is measured by promotions to greater responsibility and larger paychecks. Does God measure success in the same way? Read the following Scripture passages and comment on the portrait of success that you see.

➺ Romans 12:1-3

⮌ 1 Peter 5:5

⮌ James 4:10

⮌ Romans 2:8

⮌ Micah 6:8

⮌ Deuteronomy 28:1 (What was God's condition for blessing the nation of Israel?)

By our culture's standards, was Paul successful? Stephen? Dietrich Bonhoeffer? Mother Teresa? Whom do you know who exemplifies success in God's eyes and failure in the world's estimation? What do you admire about this person?

Application

1. Of the three successors we studied, at least two of them surely knew the day would come when their leader would be replaced. We are never told that either of them coveted the position; however, that does not mean it never crossed their minds. It simply means we don't know whether it did or it didn't. We are, however, given some information as to their character and the quality of their work.

➥ Regardless of future results, what do you think our most important aim is in our jobs?

➥ Looking at your own work habits, would you say you bring holiness to the way you do your job? Give examples, both positive and negative.

2. How did these three men prepare for their eventual promotion?

➣ Do you know anyone currently doing the kind of job you would like to have someday? If so, who? If not, how could you find someone like that?

➣ What would it take to be mentored by this person?

3. Is there any training or education you need if you are ever to attain your dream job? What is it?

➣ If so, are you willing and able to get this training or education? If the training or education is not available to you at this time, are there similar jobs you might be able to get without going back to school?

4. How do your plans line up with what God wants for you? Spend time praying for direction in your career.

Conclusion

In business, promotions are given for all sorts of reasons, and not necessarily for good ones. It's tempting to want to play the game, to get in the ring with everyone else, and do what it takes to get the job you want. But that attitude puts the focus where it doesn't belong—on your job, not your character. It isn't wrong to go after a good job. It certainly isn't wrong to plan and prepare. But along the way, don't lose sight of the real goal . . . that of holiness. And let God take care of the rest.

Memory Verse

"A good name is more desirable than great riches; to be esteemed is better than silver or gold" (Prov. 22:1).

TEN

Making a Difference

*T*he office can be an unholy place. Many Christians regard that truth as a threat, and they enter their workplace with their defenses up, ready to be persecuted and tempted, prepared to fend off the assaults of the Enemy. In some ways, that's appropriate. After all, it is easy to get sucked into the politics and gossip. We can get mowed down by the backstabbing and credit-grabbing that sometimes happens. But keep in mind, too, that most of the people you work with are not intentionally being evil; they just don't know God. As difficult as it may be sometimes for you to cope with their behavior, it's likely even more difficult for them to cope with life in general. As far as they know, they're on their own. If anything good is going to happen in their lives, they think they are the ones to make it happen. You know different—and you may be their best chance to find out the truth.

Reflection Questions

Are most of the people you work with Christian or non-Christian? What impact does this have on your work environment?

Would you say that your non-Christian coworkers can or cannot tell that there is something different in your life? Why or why not?

Introduction

We've returned to the life of Moses several times in this study guide, partly because he is one of the biblical characters we know the most about. Today we will look at bits and pieces of his story one more time as we examine some of the benefits of knowing God.

Study

Read together Numbers 12:5-8 and Exodus 33:11; 34:1-7, 29-35.

1. Moses had one great advantage over the people whom he worked with: he was able to speak with the Lord face-to-face. Why do you think he was allowed to do this?

⌒ How do you think this helped him as he carried out his job?

2. What did Moses learn about God's character?

3. When Moses had been spending time in God's presence, how was it evident to others?

Another Perspective

Moses had something that was very rare in his day—a one-on-one relationship with the Lord. Today, however, that kind of relationship is available to all of us, along with all of its benefits. Just as Moses experienced God's guidance, so can we. Let's search the Scriptures to see what else we gain by being called friends of God (John 15:15). For each verse, write the benefit implied or stated. (You'll recall some of these verses from earlier studies.)

➻ Luke 12:6-7

➻ Psalm 27:1

➻ James 1:5

➻ Colossians 2:13-14

➻ Matthew 6:25-34

≈ Hebrews 4:16

≈ Philippians 4:6-7

Application

1. When Moses spent time in the presence of God, his face shone with reflected glory. Our faces won't literally glow with God's glory, of course. But if your face often reflects worry or anger or bitterness, for example, examine your spiritual life to find out why. Our faces usually reflect what is in our hearts. What have your coworkers seen reflected on your face today?

2. Even when we know God, we can miss out on His benefits if we are not spending time with Him. What do you need most from the Lord today? (You might want to add this request to your group's prayer list.)

3. How can recognizing the void in your coworkers' lives help you to have more patience with them? Give real-life examples. (For example: When Sue makes little digs about my work or my appearance, I realize that it arises from her fear of not measuring up. She tears me down in order to feel better about herself, since there is no one in her corner telling her that she is valuable the way she is.)

4. You don't have to leave tracts on people's desks in order to help them know the Savior. What are some other ways you can be "a fragrance of Christ to God among those who are being saved and among those who are perishing" (2 Cor. 2:15, NASB)?

5. Brainstorm ways to handle the following situations:
 The people whose desks are near yours continually gossip about people as they come and go from the office. You don't normally join in, but you feel awkward and prudish staying completely out of the conversations. How can you maintain your holiness without coming across as holier-than-thou?

⤚ You've gone out for lunch with some of your coworkers. Lunch hour is over, but they show no signs of being ready to leave. You know that they have a pretty lax attitude about putting in all their hours, and you're afraid you'll give the same impression if you don't get back. Unfortunately, you didn't drive. You'd like to tell your boss it wasn't your fault, but how can you maintain your reputation without sounding like a tattletale?

⤚ You've been invited to go out with some colleagues after work this Friday. They want to see a movie that you suspect is going to be objectionable and plan to hit a few bars afterward. You don't feel comfortable with the activities they have in mind, but at the same time, you've been trying to develop a friendship with these people and this invitation feels like a step in the right direction. What should you do?

Conclusion

As Christians, our lives are not always perfect. We don't always feel God's peace, and the fruits of the Spirit are not always evident in our lives. We certainly don't always "glow." Maybe you don't feel qualified to be Christ's emissary to your workplace. Maybe you'd feel a little safer keeping your light under a bushel so that no one has to notice it flickering now and then.

But that's where God's grace comes in. We're not called to invite people to live a sinless life. We're called to show them God's mercy and His never-failing love as it is worked out in our life. That's really what it means to have holiness in the workplace.

Memory Verse

"Do everything without complaining or arguing, so that you may become blameless and pure, children of God without fault in a crooked and depraved generation, in which you shine like stars in the universe as you hold out the word of life" (Phil. 2:14-16).